Italian Cookbook for Beginners

Classic Modern Italian Dishes to Cook at Home

BY: SOPHIA FREEMAN

COPYRIGHTED

Liability

This publication is meant as an informational tool. The individual purchaser accepts all liability if damages occur because of following the directions or guidelines set out in this publication. The Author bears no responsibility for reparations caused by the misuse or misinterpretation of the content.

Copyright

The content of this publication is solely for entertainment purposes and is meant to be purchased by one individual. Permission is not given to any individual who copies, sells or distributes parts or the whole of this publication unless it is explicitly given by the Author in writing.

Table of Contents

Introduction

One of the best characteristics of Italian food is simplicity.

It is the combination of fresh ingredients and spices that are delicately seasoned to produce rich flavors.

At the heart of most Italian dishes are olive oil, tomato, basil, oregano, capers, parsley, garlic, meat or seafood, and cheese.

And don't forget the wine.

If there is something you can expect in an Italian family dinner, it's water, bread, and wine.

Most of their dishes only have a few main ingredients that will vary depending on the region.

Northern Italy cooks mostly with fish, seafood, sausages, and pork.

The North is known for its risotto (rice cooked in broth or stock), polenta (boiled cornmeal), and Parmigiano-Reggiano dubbed as "the King of Cheeses".

Central Italy focuses more on tomatoes, meats, bread, and vegetables.

This region's popular dishes are bruschetta, bisteccaalla fiorentina, and spaghetti alla carbonara.

Finally, Italy's southern region use dried pasta, seafood, and olive oil.

South Italy is known for its pizza margherita, spaghetti alle vongole, and Italian wedding soup.

Are you ready to be transported to the different regions and experience the culinary diversity of Italy?

Let's get started then!

Additional Interesting Useful Information

- Italy has a high regard for its cuisine. It finds pleasure in eating together with family and friends to relax and truly savors the food. You had better think twice to eat while walking in Italy, as it is considered disrespectful.

- "Bounappetito!" is what Italians say before enjoying a meal.

- Unlike other cultures, lunch is the main meal of the day in Italy. Italians only eat light breakfast to save their appetite and would usually consume coffee with milk in the mornings.

- Italians eat pasta at least once per day.

- The famous spaghetti and meatball is not an authentic Italian dish.

- Tomatoes and tomato sauce with pasta only came about during the 1700s

- Pizza was invented in Naples during the 18th century.

- The traditional Italian pizza has a thin crust and simple ingredients.

- Tiramisu which means "pick me up" is a famous dessert that originated in Venice.

- There are at least 600 pasta shapes and varieties in existence all over the world.

- Italians love their wine. They are the biggest producer of wine for the year 2019.

- Salads are not considered appetizers in Italy. It is eaten after the main course and has a simpler dressing that usually consists of vinegar and olive oil.

- Italy is also world-famous for its coffee.

Zucchini Caprese

Caprese is a traditional Italian salad made with tomatoes, basil, and mozzarella, drizzled with olive oil and seasoned with a little bit of salt. One interesting thing about caprese is that it features the flag colors of Italy: red, white, and green. Here's a unique twist to this salad that includes zucchini and pasta.

Serving Size: 2

Preparation Cooking Time: 20 minutes

Ingredients:

- ½ onion, chopped
- 1 tablespoon olive oil
- 2 cloves garlic, crushed and minced
- Salt and pepper to taste
- 1 zucchini, chopped
- ¼ cup mozzarella cheese, shredded
- 2 tablespoons fresh basil, chopped
- 2 tomatoes, chopped

Instructions:

1. Pour the olive oil into a pan over medium heat.

2. Cook the onion and garlic for 5 minutes, stirring frequently.

3. Sprinkle with the salt and pepper.

4. Stir in the basil and zucchini.

5. Cook for 5 minutes.

6. Top with the mozzarella cheese and tomatoes.

7. Cook for 2 minutes or until the cheese has melted.

Nutrients per Serving:

- Calories: 150.2
- Fat: 9.4 g
- Saturated Fat: 2.4 g
- Carbohydrates: 12.5 g
- Fiber: 2.9 g
- Protein: 6.1 g
- Cholesterol: 9 mg
- Sugars: 5.9 g
- Sodium: 103.4 mg
- Potassium: 518.3 mg

Italian Shrimp Risotto

Learn how to make delicious risotto with this simple and easy-to-follow recipe. Risotto is an Italian dish made by simmering rice in broth and seasoning with herbs, onion, butter, parmesan cheese, and white wine. It is a popular way to cook rice in northern Italy.

Serving Size: 4

Preparation Cooking Time: 30 minutes

Ingredients:

Shrimp

- 3 tablespoons olive oil
- Pinch red pepper flakes
- 3 cloves garlic, peeled
- 1 lb. shrimp, shelled and deveined
- 1 tablespoon lemon juice
- ½ cup dry white wine
- 1 cup parsley, chopped
- Salt and pepper to taste

Risotto

- 1 qt. fish stock
- 1 shallot, chopped
- 2 tablespoons butter
- 1 tablespoon olive oil
- ½ cup dry white wine
- 12 oz. Arborio rice

Instructions:

1. First, prepare the shrimp.

2. Add the oil to a pan over medium heat.

3. Cook the garlic for 2 minutes.

4. Stir in the shrimp.

5. Season with the red pepper flakes, salt and pepper.

6. Cook on high for 5 minutes.

7. Add the wine to the pan.

8. Scrape the browned bits using a wooden spoon.

9. Cook for 3 minutes.

10. Stir in the lemon juice and parsley.

11. Remove the garlic.

12. Remove the pan from the stove, cover and set aside.

13. Next, prepare the risotto.

14. Add the fish stock to another pan over medium heat.

15. Simmer. Set aside.

16. Add the butter to another pan over low heat.

17. Wait for it to melt.

18. Add the shallot and olive oil.

19. Cook for 3 minutes, stirring frequently.

20. Increase heat.

21. Add the rice.

22. Cook the rice until the butter and oil have been absorbed.

23. Add the fish stock and wine.

24. Stir in the shrimp.

25. Mix well.

26. Sprinkle with the parsley.

27. Let sit for 2 minutes before serving.

Nutrients per Serving:

- Calories: 702.8
- Fat: 25.4 g
- Saturated Fat: 6.5 g
- Carbohydrates: 75.2 g
- Fiber: 2.3 g
- Protein: 31 g
- Cholesterol: 125 mg
- Sugars: 1.4 g
- Sodium: 1059.1mg
- Potassium: 698.4 mg

Italian Meatballs

There are various ways of making Italian meatballs. This one is not only easy to make, but it is also scrumptious.

Serving Size: 6

Preparation Cooking Time: 50 minutes

Ingredients:

- ½ teaspoon garlic powder
- 1 ½ lb. ground beef
- ½ cup water
- 2 eggs, beaten
- ¼ cup Romano cheese, grated
- ½ teaspoon onion powder
- 1 cup breadcrumbs (Italian seasoned)
- 2 tablespoons fresh parsley, chopped
- Salt and pepper to taste

Instructions:

1. Preheat your oven to 350 degrees F.

2. In a bowl, combine all the ingredients.

3. Form meatballs from the mixture.

4. Add to a baking pan.

5. Bake in the oven for 30 minutes.

Nutrients per Serving:

- Calories: 343
- Fat: 20.4 g
- Saturated Fat: 7.8 g
- Carbohydrates: 14.1 g
- Fiber: 0.8 g
- Protein: 24.4 g
- Cholesterol: 135.2 mg
- Sugars: 1 g
- Sodium: 611.7 mg
- Potassium: 212.9 mg

Spaghetti Amatriciana

Amatriciana is another popular Italian pasta dish with a sauce made with tomato, pecorino cheese, and onion.

Serving Size: 4

Preparation Cooking Time: 30 minutes

Ingredients:

- 1 lb. spaghetti noodles, cooked
- 3 tablespoons olive oil
- 1 onion, chopped
- 7 oz. bacon, chopped
- 2 cups canned crushed tomatoes
- ½ teaspoon white sugar
- 1 tablespoon water
- 2 cups passata (crushed tomatoes)
- Pinch red pepper flakes
- Salt and pepper to taste
- 2 tablespoons Parmesan cheese, grated

Instructions:

1. Pour the olive oil into a pan over medium heat.

2. Cook the onion for 5 minutes.

3. Stir in the bacon.

4. Cook for 3 minutes.

5. Add the sugar, water and passata.

6. Stir and cook for 10 minutes.

7. Toss the spaghetti noodles in the sauce along with the red pepper flakes, salt, pepper, and Parmesan cheese.

Nutrients per Serving:

- Calories: 662.4
- Fat: 19.7 g
- Saturated Fat: 4.4 g
- Carbohydrates: 97.2 g
- Fiber: 6.5 g
- Protein: 24 g
- Cholesterol: 19.8 mg
- Sugars: 4.8 g
- Sodium: 615.7 mg
- Potassium: 749.3 mg

Lasagna

Who doesn't love lasagna? Layers of noodles, meaty sauce, cream, and herbs topped with a golden crust of melted cheese—it's every pasta lover's weakness.

Serving Size: 12

Preparation Cooking Time: 3 hours and 15 minutes

Ingredients:

- 1 white onion, minced
- 3 cloves garlic, crushed and minced
- 1 lb. lean ground beef
- 1 lb. Italian sausage, crumbled
- ½ cup water
- 13 oz. canned tomato sauce
- ½ teaspoon fennel seeds
- 12 oz. canned tomato paste
- 28 oz. canned crushed tomatoes
- 1 ½ teaspoons dried basil
- 2 tablespoons sugar
- 1 teaspoon Italian seasoning
- 4 tablespoons fresh parsley, chopped
- Salt and pepper to taste
- 1 egg, beaten
- 16 oz. ricotta cheese
- 12 lasagna noodles, cooked
- 1 lb. mozzarella cheese, sliced
- ¾ cup Parmesan cheese, grated

Instructions:

1. Add the onion, garlic, ground beef and sausage to a pan over medium heat.

2. Cook for 3 to 5 minutes or until meat is brown.

3. Pour in the water, tomato sauce, tomato paste and crushed tomatoes.

4. Sprinkle with the basil, sugar, Italian seasoning, fennel seeds, parsley, salt and pepper.

5. Simmer for 1 hour and 30 minutes, stirring from time to time.

6. In a bowl, mix the egg and ricotta.

7. Preheat your oven to 375 degrees F.

8. Spread the meat sauce on the bottom of a baking pan.

9. Arrange the lasagna noodles on top of the meat sauce.

10. Spread with some of the ricotta mixture.

11. Top with the mozzarella cheese.

12. Repeat the layers.

13. Top with the Parmesan cheese.

14. Cover the baking pan with foil.

15. Bake in the oven for 20 minutes.

16. Uncover and bake for another 30 minutes.

17. Let cool for a few minutes before serving.

Nutrients per Serving:

- Calories: 448
- Fat: 21.3 g
- Saturated Fat: 10.0 g
- Carbohydrates: 36.5 g
- Fiber: 4 g
- Protein: 29.7 g
- Cholesterol: 82 mg
- Sugars: 9 g
- Sodium: 1400 mg
- Potassium: 876 mg

Pork Piccata

Piccata is an Italian dish made of thinly sliced pork, beef, or veal meat, covered with flour and sautéed. It is usually served with lemon butter sauce. In this recipe, we will make use of pork chops, flattened with a meat mallet.

Serving Size: 4

Preparation Cooking Time: 45 minutes

Ingredients:

- 4 pork chops
- Salt and pepper to taste
- ½ cup all-purpose flour
- 3 tablespoons butter
- 2 tablespoons shallots, chopped
- ¼ cup chicken broth
- ⅓ cup dry white wine
- 1 tablespoon freshly squeezed lemon juice
- ¼ cup fresh parsley, chopped
- 1 tablespoon lemon zest
- 1 tablespoon capers

Instructions:

1. Preheat your oven to 300 degrees F.

2. Place a wax paper on top of the pork chop and then pound with a meat mallet until it is only 1/8 inch thin.

3. In a bowl, mix the salt, pepper, and flour.

4. Dredge the pork chops with this mixture.

5. Add the butter to a pan over medium heat.

6. Once melted, add the pork chops and shallots.

7. Cook for 3 minutes per side or until golden.

8. Transfer to a baking dish.

9. Bake in the oven for 20 minutes.

10. Add the broth and wine to the pan.

11. Scrape the browned bits using a wooden spoon.

12. Reduce heat.

13. Simmer for 5 minutes.

14. Add the lemon juice to the sauce.

15. Pour the sauce over the pork chops.

16. Sprinkle the lemon zest, parsley, and capers on top.

Nutrients per Serving:

- Calories: 321.2
- Fat: 15.8 g
- Saturated Fat: 8 g
- Carbohydrates: 14.3 g
- Fiber: 0.8 g
- Protein: 25.6 g
- Cholesterol: 81.9 mg
- Sugars: 0.6 g
- Sodium: 184.6 mg
- Potassium: 420 mg

Chicken Parmesan

Also called chicken Parmigiana, chicken Parmesan is made by dredging chicken with breadcrumbs, baking, or frying it until golden, covering it in tomato sauce and topping it with cheese. Make it at home using this easy and simple recipe.

Serving Size: 4

Preparation Cooking Time: 1 hour

Ingredients:

- 2 tablespoons all-purpose flour
- 4 chicken breast fillets
- Salt and pepper to taste
- ½ cup tomato sauce
- 2 eggs, beaten
- ½ cup Parmesan cheese, grated
- 1 cup panko breadcrumbs
- 1 cup olive oil for frying
- ¼ cup basil, chopped
- ¼ cup mozzarella, sliced into small cubes
- ½ cup provolone cheese, grated

Instructions:

1. Preheat your oven to 450 degrees F.

2. Place the chicken breasts on your kitchen table.

3. Pound the chicken with a meat mallet to make it thinner.

4. Season with the salt and pepper.

5. In another bowl, combine half of the Parmesan cheese and breadcrumbs.

6. Coat the chicken with the flour, and then dip in egg.

7. Dredge with the breadcrumb mixture.

8. Pour the olive oil into a pan over medium heat.

9. Once hot, add the chicken and cook for 2 to 3 minutes per side.

10. Transfer to a baking pan.

11. Top with the tomato sauce, basil, and cheese.

12. Bake in the oven for 20 minutes or until the cheese has melted and turned a little brown in the center.

Nutrients per Serving:

- Calories: 470.8
- Fat: 24.9 g
- Saturated Fat: 9.1 g
- Carbohydrates: 24.8 g
- Protein: 42.1 g
- Fiber: 0.6 g
- Cholesterol: 186.7 mg
- Sugars: 1.7 g
- Sodium: 840.3 mg
- Potassium: 388.9 mg

Eggplant Parmesan

In this version of eggplant Parmesan, the dish is baked instead of fried. But still, the results are too enticing to resist.

Serving Size: 10

Preparation Cooking Time: 1 hour

Ingredients:

- 3 eggplant, sliced thinly lengthwise
- 2 eggs, beaten
- 4 cups breadcrumbs
- 6 cups tomato sauce
- 16 oz. mozzarella cheese
- ½ cup Parmesan cheese
- Dried basil

Instructions:

1. Preheat your oven to 350 degrees F.

2. Dip the eggplant in beaten egg.

3. Dredge with the breadcrumbs.

4. Add these to a baking pan.

5. Bake in the oven for 5 minutes.

6. Flip and bake for another 5 minutes.

7. In another baking pan, add the tomato sauce and spread.

8. Add the eggplant slices.

9. Top with the cheeses and basil.

10. Bake in the oven for 30 to 35 minutes.

Nutrients per Serving:

- Calories: 487.4
- Fat: 16 g
- Saturated Fat: 6.7 g
- Carbohydrates: 62.1 g
- Fiber: 8.8 g
- Protein: 24.2 g
- Cholesterol: 72.8 mg
- Sugars: 19.9 g
- Sodium: 1663.1 mg
- Potassium: 815.4 mg

Sausage Soup

This Italian sausage soup is not only full of flavor but also very easy to make. It's a perfect addition to any meal.

Serving Size: 6

Preparation Cooking Time: 50 minutes

Ingredients:

- 2 cloves garlic, minced
- 1 lb. Italian sausage, crumbled
- 15 oz. Italian stewed tomatoes
- 1 cup carrots, sliced
- 28 oz. beef broth
- Salt and pepper to taste
- 15 oz. great Northern beans
- 2 zucchini, sliced into cubes
- 2 cups spinach, chopped

Instructions:

1. In a pot over medium heat, cook the garlic and sausage for 3 to 5 minutes or until sausage is browned.

2. Add the tomatoes, carrots, and broth.

3. Sprinkle with the salt and pepper.

4. Reduce heat and simmer for 15 minutes.

5. Add the beans and zucchini.

6. Simmer for 15 minutes.

7. Stir in the spinach.

8. Cook for 5 minutes.

Nutrients per Serving:

- Calories: 385
- Fat: 24.4 g
- Saturated Fat: 9.0 g
- Carbohydrates: 22.5 g
- Fiber: 5.7 g
- Protein: 18.8 g
- Cholesterol: 58 mg
- Sugars: 4 g
- Sodium: 1259 mg
- Potassium: 810 mg

Mushroom Risotto

Here's another tasty way of preparing risotto—with mushrooms, herbs, butter, and Parmesan cheese. For sure, you and your family will love this.

Serving Size: 6

Preparation Cooking Time: 50 minutes

Ingredients:

- 6 cups low-sodium chicken broth, divided
- 1 lb. Portobello mushrooms, sliced thinly
- 1 lb. button mushrooms, chopped
- 2 shallots, chopped
- ½ cup dry white wine
- 1 ½ cups Arborio rice
- 3 tablespoons olive oil, divided
- Salt and pepper to taste
- 3 tablespoons chives, chopped
- ⅓ cup Parmesan cheese, grated
- 4 tablespoons butter

Instructions:

1. In a pan over medium low heat, simmer the broth until heated.

2. Pour half of the oil into another pan over medium heat.

3. Add the mushrooms and cook for 3 minutes.

4. Transfer to a plate and set aside.

5. Add the remaining oil to the pan.

6. Cook the rice and shallots for 2 minutes, stirring often.

7. Pour in the wine and stir.

8. Add half of the broth to the pan.

9. Stir until fully absorbed.

10. Cook while stirring for 15 minutes.

11. Add the mushrooms and the rest of the ingredients.

12. Season with the salt and pepper.

Nutrients per Serving:

- Calories: 430.6
- Fat: 16.6 g
- Saturated Fat: 6.6 g
- Carbohydrates: 56.6 g
- Fiber: 2.7 g
- Protein: 11.3 g
- Cholesterol: 29.3 mg
- Sugars: 4.4 g
- Sodium: 1130.8 mg
- Potassium: 692 mg

Spaghetti with Meatballs

Italian spaghetti is popular all over the world. It has so many variations, it's hard to know which one is authentic. Here's another way of making Italian spaghetti, and it's topped with delicious meatballs.

Serving Size: 6

Preparation Cooking Time: 2 hours and 20 minutes

Ingredients:

Meatballs

- 1 lb. lean ground beef
- ⅛ teaspoon garlic powder
- 1 tablespoon dried parsley
- 1 cup breadcrumbs
- 1 egg, beaten
- 1 tablespoon Parmesan cheese, grated
- Pepper to taste
- Noodles and Sauce
- ¼ cup olive oil
- 1 cup onion, chopped
- 5 cloves garlic, crushed and minced
- 6 oz. canned tomato paste
- 56 oz. canned whole tomatoes
- ¾ teaspoon dried basil
- 1 teaspoon white sugar
- 1 bay leaf
- Salt and pepper to taste
- 6 cups spaghetti noodles, cooked

Instructions:

1. Combine the ground beef, garlic powder, dried parsley, breadcrumbs, egg, Parmesan cheese and pepper in a bowl.

2. Mix and then form meatballs from the mixture.

3. Cover in cling wrap and place in the refrigerator.

4. In a pan over medium heat, add the olive oil.

5. Cook the onion and garlic for 2 to 3 minutes.

6. Stir in the tomato paste, tomatoes, basil, sugar, bay leaf, salt and pepper.

7. Cover and reduce heat.

8. Simmer for 90 minutes.

9. Stir in the meatballs.

10. Remove from heat.

11. Toss the spaghetti noodles in the sauce and meatballs.

Nutrients per Serving:

- Calories: 346.6
- Fat: 21.2 g
- Saturated Fat: 5.9 g
- Carbohydrates: 23 g
- Fiber: 4.5 g
- Protein: 18.9 g
- Cholesterol: 77.4 mg
- Sugars: 11.1 g
- Sodium: 1492.5 mg
- Potassium: 1023.1 mg

Chicken Milanese

This chicken and pasta dish is unforgettable. It's made flavorful thanks to the garlic, fresh basil leaves, and sun-dried tomatoes. You can make the sauce a day ahead.

Serving Size: 4

Preparation Cooking Time: 30 minutes

Ingredients:

- ½ cup sun-dried tomatoes, minced
- 2 cloves garlic, crushed and minced
- 1 tablespoon butter
- 1 cup chicken broth, divided
- 1 cup heavy cream
- 1 lb. chicken breast fillet
- Salt and pepper to taste
- 2 tablespoons vegetable oil
- 2 tablespoons fresh basil leaves, chopped
- 8 oz. fettuccini pasta, cooked

Instructions:

1. First, in a pan over medium heat, add the butter and garlic.

2. Cook for 30 seconds, stirring frequently.

3. Stir in the tomato and 3/4 cup chicken broth.

4. Bring to a boil.

5. Reduce heat and simmer for 10 minutes.

6. Stir in the cream.

7. Increase heat.

8. Bring to a boil and then reduce heat.

9. Simmer for 5 minutes.

10. Season the chicken with the salt and pepper.

11. In another pan over medium heat, add the oil and cook the chicken.

12. Cook for 4 minutes per side.

13. Transfer to a bowl.

14. In the same pan, add the remaining broth.

15. Add this to the cream sauce.

16. Sprinkle with the basil.

17. Toss the pasta in the sauce and top with the chicken.

Nutrients per Serving:

- Calories: 640.8
- Fat: 34.8 g
- Saturated Fat: 17.1 g
- Carbohydrates: 47 g
- Fiber: 2.8 g
- Protein: 36.3 g
- Cholesterol: 156.3 mg
- Sugars: 4.7 g
- Sodium: 501.5 mg
- Potassium: 681.2 mg

Italian Pork Chops

Italian-style pork chops are dredged first with a combination of Parmesan cheese and parsley before frying in oil to give them beautiful golden brown finish.

Serving Size: 4

Preparation Cooking Time: 1 hour

Ingredients:

- 3 tablespoons milk
- ½ cup Parmesan cheese, grated
- 2 tablespoons dried parsley
- 3 eggs, beaten
- 1 ½ cups breadcrumbs
- 2 tablespoons olive oil
- 4 cloves garlic, minced
- 4 pork chops

Instructions:

1. Preheat your oven to 325 degrees F.

2. In a bowl, combine the milk and eggs.

3. In another bowl, mix the Parmesan cheese, parsley, and breadcrumbs.

4. Pour the oil into a pan over medium heat.

5. Add the garlic and cook for 1 minute, stirring often.

6. Remove the garlic from the oil.

7. Dip the pork chop in the eggs.

8. Dredge with the breadcrumbs.

9. Add to the pan and cook for 5 minutes per side or until golden.

10. Transfer to the oven.

11. Bake for 25 minutes.

Nutrients per Serving:

- Calories: 440
- Fat: 20.3 g
- Saturated Fat: 6.0 g
- Carbohydrates: 33.4 g
- Fiber: 2.5 g
- Protein: 30 g
- Cholesterol: 186 mg
- Sugars: 4g
- Sodium: 1026 mg
- Potassium: 429 mg

Shrimp Alfredo

It only takes a few minutes to whip up this special pasta dish—penne pasta drenched in a creamy sauce and topped with shrimp and parsley.

Serving Size: 6

Preparation Cooking Time: 50 minutes

Ingredients:

- 2 tablespoons olive oil
- ¼ cup butter
- 1 onion, diced
- 2 cloves garlic, minced
- ½ lb. Portobello mushrooms, sliced
- 1 red bell pepper, chopped
- 1 lb. shrimp, shelled and deveined
- 15 oz. Alfredo sauce
- ½ cup Romano cheese, grated
- ½ cup cream
- Pinch cayenne pepper
- Salt and pepper to taste
- 12 oz. penne pasta, cooked according to package directions

Instructions:

1. Add the olive oil and butter to a pan over medium heat.

2. Cook the onion and garlic for 2 to 3 minutes, stirring often.

3. Add the mushrooms and red bell pepper.

4. Cook for 2 minutes.

5. Add the shrimp.

6. Pour in the cream and Alfredo sauce.

7. Stir in the cheese.

8. Simmer for 5 minutes or until the sauce has thickened.

9. Season with the salt, pepper, and cayenne.

10. Toss the pasta in the sauce and top with the parsley.

Nutrients per Serving:

- Calories: 707
- Fat: 45 g
- Saturated Fat: 20.3 g
- Carbohydrates: 50.6 g
- Fiber: 3.4 g
- Protein: 28.4 g
- Cholesterol: 201.5 mg
- Sugars: 6.6 g
- Sodium: 1034.5 mg
- Potassium: 513.5 mg

Chicken Alfredo

If you're not fond of seafood, you can use chicken instead of shrimp to flavor up your Alfredo pasta.

Serving Size: 8

Preparation Cooking Time: 1 hour

Ingredients:

- 6 chicken breast fillets, sliced into cubes
- 6 tablespoons butter, divided
- 6 cloves garlic, minced, divided
- 1 tablespoon Italian seasoning
- 1 onion, chopped
- 8 oz. mushrooms, sliced
- ¾ cup Parmesan cheese, grated
- Salt and pepper to taste
- ½ cup all-purpose flour
- 1 cup half-and-half
- 3 cups milk
- 8 oz. Colby-Monterey Jack cheese, shredded
- ½ cup sour cream
- 1 lb. fettuccini pasta, cooked according to package directions
- 3 tomatoes, chopped

Instructions:

1. Add half of the butter to a pan over medium heat.

2. Season the chicken with the Italian seasoning.

3. Add half of the garlic and chicken to the pan and cook for 3 to 4 minutes per side.

4. Remove from heat and set aside.

5. In another pan, add the remaining butter along with the remaining garlic, onion, and mushrooms.

6. Stir in the salt, pepper, and flour.

7. Cook for 2 minutes.

8. Stir in the half-and-half and milk.

9. Add the cheeses, sour cream, and tomatoes.

10. Turn off the heat.

11. Toss the pasta in the sauce.

12. Top with the chicken.

Nutrients per Serving:

- Calories: 672.9
- Fat: 30.8 g
- Saturated Fat: 18.9 g
- Carbohydrates: 57 g
- Fiber: 3.2 g
- Protein: 43.3 g
- Cholesterol: 132.8 mg
- Sugars: 8.2 g
- Sodium: 1385.9 mg
- Potassium: 732 mg

Chicken Piccata with Lemon

This chicken piccata dish seems fancy, but it's actually easy to prepare.

Serving Size: 4

Preparation Cooking Time: 50 minutes

Ingredients:

- 3 chicken breast fillets, sliced into medallions
- Salt and pepper to taste
- ½ cup all-purpose flour
- 2 tablespoons vegetable oil
- 2 cloves garlic, crushed and minced
- 2 tablespoons capers, rinsed and drained
- 1 lemon, sliced thinly
- ¼ cup freshly squeezed lemon juice
- 1 cup of reduced-sodium chicken broth
- 3 tablespoons butter
- 2 tablespoons parsley, minced

Instructions:

1. Preheat your oven to 200 degrees F.

2. Sprinkle both sides of the chicken with the salt and pepper.

3. Coat with the flour.

4. Add the oil to a pan over medium heat.

5. Fry the chicken for 3 minutes per side or until golden.

6. Place the chicken on a strainer.

7. Add the garlic to the pan.

8. Cook for 20 seconds, stirring frequently.

9. Add the chicken broth.

10. Scrape the browned bits using a wooden spoon.

11. Add the lemon slices.

12. Bring to a boil.

13. Reduce heat and simmer for 8 to 10 minutes.

14. Stir in the capers and lemon juice.

15. Simmer for 5 minutes.

16. Add the butter and parsley.

17. Place the chicken on a serving platter.

18. Pour the sauce over the chicken and serve.

Nutrients per Serving:

- Calories: 421
- Fat: 21.2 g
- Saturated Fat: 8.2 g
- Carbohydrates: 16.1 g
- Fiber: 1.3 g
- Protein: 41.1 g
- Cholesterol: 127.6 mg
- Sugars: 0.7 g
- Sodium: 347.9 mg
- Potassium: 387.7 mg

Italian Sausage with Peppers Onions

Although this recipe is simple to prepare, the result is a dish that would make you feel like you're in a fancy restaurant.

Serving Size: 6

Preparation Cooking Time: 40 minutes

Ingredients:

- 6 links Italian sausage
- 2 tablespoons butter
- 1 white onion, sliced thinly
- ½ onion, sliced
- 4 cloves garlic, minced
- 1 green bell pepper, sliced thinly
- 1 red bell pepper, sliced thinly
- ¼ cup white wine
- 1 teaspoon dried oregano
- 1 teaspoon dried basil

Instructions:

1. Add the sausage to a pan over medium heat.

2. Cook the sausage until brown on all sides.

3. Transfer to a cutting board and slice.

4. Add the butter to a pan over medium heat.

5. Cook the onions and garlic for 3 minutes.

6. Stir in the bell peppers, wine, and herbs.

7. Add the sausage to the pan.

8. Mix well.

9. Reduce heat.

10. Simmer for 15 minutes.

Nutrients per Serving:

- Calories: 461
- Fat: 39.4 g
- Saturated Fat: 15 g
- Carbohydrates: 7 g
- Fiber: 1.6 g
- Protein: 17.1 g
- Cholesterol: 96 mg
- Sugars: 3 g
- Sodium: 857 mg
- Potassium: 445 mg

Salami Pepperoni Pasta Salad

This pasta salad is a delicious combination of seashell pasta, dressing, salami, pepperoni, and cheese.

Serving Size: 12

Preparation Cooking Time: 1 hour and 40 minutes

Ingredients:

- ¼ lb. pepperoni sausage, chopped
- ¼ lb. salami, chopped
- 3 tomatoes, chopped
- 1 red bell pepper, chopped
- 1 green bell pepper, chopped
- 6 oz. black olives, sliced
- ½ lb. Asiago cheese, sliced into cubes
- 1 lb. seashell pasta, cooked according to package directions
- 1 oz. Italian dressing mix
- ¼ cup balsamic vinegar
- ¾ cup olive oil
- 2 tablespoons dried oregano
- 1 tablespoon dried parsley
- 1 tablespoon Parmesan cheese, grated
- Salt and pepper to taste

Instructions:

1. Add the pepperoni, salami, tomatoes, bell peppers, black olives, cheese, and pasta in a large bowl.

2. Sprinkle the Italian dressing mix on top.

3. Mix well.

4. Cover the bowl and refrigerate for 1 hour.

5. Prepare the dressing by mixing the vinegar, olive oil, dried herbs, Parmesan cheese, salt, and pepper.

6. Pour the dressing into the salad.

7. Toss to coat evenly.

8. Serve immediately.

Nutrients per Serving:

- Calories: 451
- Fat: 29.1 g
- Saturated Fat: 8.2 g
- Carbohydrates: 33.2 g
- Fiber: 2.8 g
- Protein: 15 g
- Cholesterol: 36.6 mg
- Sugars: 4.3 g
- Sodium: 977.5 mg
- Potassium: 266.6 mg

Baked Chicken

Once you've tried preparing chicken this way, you'll probably hardly ever fry it again. The mixture of mayo, garlic powder, and Parmesan cheese adds interesting flavors to chicken.

Serving Size: 4

Preparation Cooking Time: 30 minutes

Ingredients:

- 1 cup light mayonnaise
- ½ cup Parmesan cheese, grated
- 1 teaspoon garlic powder
- 1 cup breadcrumbs
- 4 chicken breast fillets

Instructions:

1. Preheat your oven to 425 degrees F.

2. In a bowl, combine the mayo, garlic powder and Parmesan cheese.

3. Add the breadcrumbs to another bowl.

4. Dip the chicken into the mayo mixture.

5. Dredge with the breadcrumbs.

6. Arrange in a single layer on a baking pan.

7. Bake for 20 minutes or until golden.

Nutrients per Serving:

- Calories: 553.9
- Fat: 39.6 g
- Saturated Fat: 7.4 g
- Carbohydrates: 17.1 g
- Fiber: 0.8 g
- Protein: 31.8 g
- Cholesterol: 91.6 mg
- Sugars: 1.4 g
- Sodium: 768.3 mg
- Potassium: 225.4 mg

Creamy Shrimp Pesto

Pesto is a simple pasta sauce made by blending basil leaves, walnuts or pine nuts, garlic, Parmesan cheese, and olive oil. We add a little twist to the usual pesto pasta by throwing in some shrimp and cream into the mix.

Serving Size: 8

Preparation Cooking Time: 30 minutes

Ingredients:

- 1 lb. linguine pasta, cooked according to package directions
- ½ cup butter
- 2 cups heavy cream
- Pepper to taste
- 1 cup Parmesan cheese, grated
- ⅓ cup pesto sauce
- 1 lb. shrimp, shelled and deveined

Instructions:

1. In a pan over medium heat, add the butter and cream.

2. Season with the pepper.

3. Cook for 6 minutes, stirring frequently.

4. Add the Parmesan cheese.

5. Stir well.

6. Add the pesto and cook for 4 minutes.

7. Add the shrimp and cook for 5 minutes.

8. Toss the pasta in the sauce and serve.

Nutrients per Serving:

- Calories: 646
- Fat: 42.5 g
- Saturated Fat: 24.3 g
- Carbohydrates: 43 g
- Fiber: 2.7 g
- Protein: 23.1 g
- Cholesterol: 210.4 mg
- Sugars: 0.2 g
- Sodium: 437.2 mg
- Potassium: 217 mg

Focaccia Bread

Focaccia is a type of Italian bread that looks like pizza dough. It is commonly served as an appetizer, snack, or antipasto.

Serving Size: 12

Preparation Cooking Time: 1 hour

Ingredients:

- 2 ¾ cups all-purpose flour
- 1 tablespoon vegetable oil
- 1 tablespoon active dry yeast
- 1 teaspoon white sugar
- ½ teaspoon dried basil
- 1 teaspoon dried thyme
- 1 teaspoon dried oregano
- 1 teaspoon garlic powder
- Salt and pepper to taste
- 1 cup water
- 2 tablespoons olive oil
- 1 cup mozzarella
- 1 tablespoon Parmesan cheese, grated

Instructions:

1. Combine the flour, vegetable oil, yeast, sugar, dried herbs, garlic powder, salt, pepper, and water.

2. Mix well.

3. Knead the dough on your kitchen table until smooth.

4. Coat the dough with oil.

5. Wrap it with a damp cloth.

6. Let it rise for 20 minutes.

7. Preheat your oven to 450 degrees F.

8. Press the dough onto a baking pan.

9. Brush the top of the dough with the oil.

10. Sprinkle the mozzarella cheese and Parmesan cheese on top.

11. Bake in the oven for 15 to 20 minutes.

Nutrients per Serving:

- Calories: 170.6
- Fat: 5.8 g
- Saturated Fat: 1.8 g
- Carbohydrates: 23.4 g
- Fiber: 1.1 g
- Protein: 6 g
- Cholesterol: 5.4 mg
- Sugars: 0.5 g
- Sodium: 252.5 mg
- Potassium: 68.9 mg

Tuscan Soup

In Italy, this soup dish is called "zuppa toscana". The traditional Tuscan soup is made with carrots, kale, onion, tomato pulp, chili powder, zucchini, kale, potatoes, celery, and cannellini beans. Here's another way of making Tuscan soup that you'll surely love.

Serving Size: 4

Preparation Cooking Time: 50 minutes

Ingredients:

- 1 onion, minced
- 3 Italian sausage links, removed from casing and crumbled
- 3 potatoes, sliced into cubes
- 6 cups reduced-sodium chicken broth
- 1 cup spinach, chopped
- ¼ cup evaporated milk
- Salt and pepper to taste

Instructions:

1. Add the onion and sausage in a pan over medium heat.

2. Cook until the sausage is browned.

3. Drain the fat and then transfer the sausage and onion to a soup pot.

4. Add the potatoes and broth.

5. Boil until the potatoes are tender.

6. Stir in the spinach.

7. Cook for 3 minutes.

8. Turn off the heat.

9. Pour in the milk and season with the salt and pepper before serving.

Nutrients per Serving:

- Calories: 558.5
- Fat: 25.2 g
- Saturated Fat: 9.1 g
- Carbohydrates: 57.4 g
- Fiber: 8.4 g
- Protein: 26.4 g
- Cholesterol: 56.4 mg
- Sugars: 6.3 g
- Sodium: 1745.3 mg
- Potassium: 2209.6 mg

Cheesy Pesto Chicken

Cut back on the usual fried chicken and prepare your chicken this way. Stuff it with cheese, pesto sauce, and herbs, and the result is definitely unforgettable.

Serving Size: 4

Preparation Cooking Time: 1 hour and 10 minutes

Ingredients:

- 1 cooking spray
- 4 chicken breast fillet, flattened
- 1 cup basil pesto
- 4 slices mozzarella cheese

Instructions:

1. Preheat your oven to 350 degrees F.

2. Spray your baking pan with oil.

3. Place the chicken fillets on top of your kitchen table.

4. Spread the pesto sauce on top of the chicken.

5. Put the cheese on top of the pesto.

6. Roll up the chicken fillets.

7. Secure using toothpicks.

8. Arrange in the baking pan.

9. Bake in the oven for 50 minutes.

Nutrients per Serving:

- Calories: 585.3
- Fat: 40.3 g
- Saturated Fat: 14.2 g
- Carbohydrates: 5.6 g
- Fiber: 1.8 g
- Protein: 49.5 g
- Cholesterol: 123.5 mg
- Sugars: 0.6 g
- Sodium: 886.1 mg
- Potassium: 431.6 mg

Rosemary Roast Chicken

Roast chicken can be made in so many ways. Here's one that will surely be a hit in the dinner table. It only requires a few ingredients to get this dish done.

Serving Size: 6

Preparation Cooking Time: 2 hours and 10 minutes

Ingredients:

- 1 whole chicken
- ¼ cup fresh rosemary, chopped
- 1 onion, sliced into wedges
- Salt and pepper to taste

Instructions:

1. Preheat your oven to 350 degrees F.

2. Add the rosemary and onion inside the chicken.

3. Sprinkle the salt and pepper all over the chicken.

4. Add the chicken to a baking pan.

5. Roast in the oven for 2 hours.

Nutrients per Serving:

- Calories: 290.8
- Fat: 17.2 g
- Saturated Fat: 4.8 g
- Carbohydrates: 1.3 g
- Fiber: 0.4 g
- Protein: 30.8 g
- Cholesterol: 97 mg
- Sugars: 0.5 g
- Sodium: 94 mg
- Potassium: 294 mg

Modonese Pork Chop

A surprisingly easy recipe that you'd love to prepare more often at home—Modonese pork chops seasoned with rosemary and garlic and cooked with white wine.

Serving Size: 4

Preparation Cooking Time: 40 minutes

Ingredients:

- 4 tablespoons butter
- 4 pork chops
- ½ white wine
- 2 cloves garlic, crushed and minced
- 1 teaspoon dried rosemary
- Salt and pepper to taste

Instructions:

1. Add the butter to a pan over medium heat.

2. Cook the pork chops for 3 minutes per side or until golden brown on both sides.

3. Add the wine.

4. Stir in the garlic, rosemary, salt and pepper.

5. Simmer for 20 minutes.

6. Pour the sauce over the pork chops and serve.

Nutrients per Serving:

- Calories: 297
- Fat: 19.2 g
- Saturated Fat: 10.0 g
- Cholesterol: 88 mg
- Carbohydrates: 1.5 g
- Fiber: 0.1 g
- Protein: 23.2 g
- Sugars: 0 g
- Sodium: 698 mg
- Potassium: 362 mg

Tofu Parmigiana

If you love eggplant Parmesan, why don't you give this recipe a try? Instead of eggplant, tofu slices are drenched with savory tomato sauce and topped with melted cheese.

Serving Size: 4

Preparation Cooking Time: 45 minutes

Ingredients:

- ½ cup breadcrumbs
- 2 teaspoons dried oregano, divided
- Salt and pepper to taste
- 5 tablespoons Parmesan cheese, grated
- 12 oz. tofu, sliced
- 2 tablespoons olive oil
- ½ teaspoon dried basil
- 8 oz. canned tomato sauce
- 1 clove garlic, minced
- 4 oz. mozzarella cheese, shredded

Instructions:

1. Combine the breadcrumbs, half of dried oregano, salt, pepper, and Parmesan cheese.

2. Coat the tofu with the breadcrumb mixture.

3. Pour the oil into a pan over medium heat.

4. Cook the tofu until golden on both sides.

5. In a bowl, mix the remaining oregano, dried basil, tomato sauce and garlic.

6. Spread the sauce in a baking pan.

7. Place the tofu slices on top of the sauce.

8. Sprinkle the mozzarella cheese on top.

9. Bake in the oven for 400 degrees for 20 minutes.

Nutrients per Serving:

- Calories: 356.9
- Fat: 21.5 g
- Saturated Fat: 6.2 g
- Carbohydrates: 18.8 g
- Fiber: 3.9 g
- Protein: 25.7 g
- Cholesterol: 23.8 mg
- Sugars: 3.5 g
- Sodium: 840.7 mg
- Potassium: 475.2 mg

Penne Arrabbiata

Want to have some zinc in your pasta? Why don't you give this penne arrabbiata recipe a try? Penne is drenched in arrabbiata sauce, spicy tomato sauce mixed with olive oil, garlic, red chili peppers, and herbs. It originated in the Lazio region near Rome, Italy.

Serving Size: 4

Preparation Cooking Time: 40 minutes

Ingredients:

- ½ cup olive oil, divided
- 6 cloves garlic, sliced
- 1 teaspoon red pepper flakes
- ½ cup tomato sauce
- 1 cup fresh basil leaves, chopped
- 28 oz. canned diced tomatoes
- 12 oz. penne pasta, cooked according to package directions
- 2 cups breadcrumbs
- 2 eggs, beaten
- 1 teaspoon garlic powder
- Salt and pepper to taste
- 1 lb. chicken breast fillet, sliced

Instructions:

1. Pour half of the olive into a pan over medium heat.

2. Cook the garlic for 2 minutes.

3. Add the red pepper flakes to the pan.

4. Cook for another 1 minute.

5. Stir in the tomato sauce, basil, and canned tomatoes.

6. Simmer for 20 minutes, stirring from time to time.

7. Add the breadcrumbs to a bowl.

8. Pour in the eggs to another bowl.

9. Dip the chicken in the eggs and then dredge with the breadcrumbs.

10. Add the remaining oil to a pan over medium heat.

11. Cook the chicken until golden on both sides.

12. Transfer the chicken to a cutting board and slice.

13. Toss the pasta in the arrabbiata sauce.

14. Top with the chicken and serve.

Nutrients per Serving:

- Calories: 587.9
- Fat: 16.5 g
- Saturated Fat: 3.2 g
- Carbohydrates: 75.3 g
- Fiber: 5.5 g
- Protein: 33.6 g
- Cholesterol: 108.1 mg
- Sugars: 8.6 g
- Sodium: 1034.2 mg
- Potassium: 644 mg

Italian Cod

Here's a light, filling, and delicious fish recipe that only takes a few minutes to prepare.

Serving Size: 4

Preparation Cooking Time: 30 minutes

Ingredients:

- ¼ cup breadcrumbs
- 1 tablespoon cornmeal
- 2 tablespoons Parmesan cheese, grated
- ⅛ teaspoon garlic powder
- ½ teaspoon Italian seasoning
- Pepper to taste
- 1 teaspoon olive oil
- Cooking spray
- 4 cod fillets
- 1 egg, beaten

Instructions:

1. Preheat your oven to 450 degrees F.

2. In a bowl, combine the breadcrumbs, cornmeal, Parmesan cheese, garlic powder, Italian seasoning, pepper, and olive oil.

3. Coat the fish with egg and then dredge with breadcrumb mixture.

4. Spray your broiler pan with oil.

5. Add the fish to the pan.

6. Bake in the oven for 12 to 15 minutes.

Nutrients per Serving:

- Calories: 130.7
- Fat: 2.9 g
- Saturated Fat: 0.8 g
- Carbohydrates: 7 g
- Fiber: 0.5 g
- Protein: 18.1 g
- Cholesterol: 38.8 mg
- Sugars: 0.6 g
- Sodium: 147.7 mg
- Potassium: 389.2 mg

Chicken Cacciatore

This Italian dish can also be prepared by using a rabbit. But if you're not up for that, here's a recipe that uses a chicken instead.

Serving Size: 6

Preparation Cooking Time: 8 hours and 15 minutes

Ingredients:

- 6 chicken breast fillet
- 28 oz. spaghetti sauce
- 1 onion, chopped
- 4 cloves garlic, crushed and minced
- 2 green bell pepper, chopped
- 8 oz. mushrooms, sliced

Instructions:

1. Add the chicken to your slow cooker.

2. Pour in the spaghetti sauce.

3. Stir in the onion, garlic, green bell pepper and mushrooms.

4. Cover the pot.

5. Cook on low for 8 hours.

Nutrients per Serving:

- Calories: 260.6
- Fat: 6.1 g
- Saturated Fat: 1.6 g
- Carbohydrates: 23.7 g
- Fiber: 4.8 g
- Protein: 27.1 g
- Cholesterol: 63.4 mg
- Sugars: 13.9 g
- Sodium: 589.8 mg
- Potassium: 786.8 mg

Manicotti

Manicotti is a pasta dish usually made with large pasta tubes stuffed with meat and spinach filling, sprinkled with cheese on top, and then baked.

Serving Size: 4

Preparation Cooking Time: 1 hour

Ingredients:

- 2 eggs, beaten
- 8 oz. mozzarella cheese, shredded
- 1 pint ricotta cheese
- ¾ cup Parmesan cheese, grated and divided
- Salt and pepper to taste
- 1 teaspoon dried parsley
- 16 oz. spaghetti sauce, divided
- 5 ½ oz. manicotti pasta, cooked according to pasta directions

Instructions:

1. Preheat your oven to 350 degrees F.

2. Mix the eggs, mozzarella cheese, ricotta cheese, half of Parmesan cheese, salt, pepper, and dried parsley.

3. Spread half of the spaghetti sauce on the baking pan.

4. Stuff the pasta dubs with the mixture.

5. Place on top of the sauce.

6. Spread the remaining spaghetti sauce on top of the pasta.

7. Top with the remaining Parmesan cheese.

8. Bake in the oven for 45 minutes.

Nutrients per Serving:

- Calories: 676.3
- Fat: 30.9 g
- Saturated Fat: 17.1 g
- Carbohydrates: 53.2 g
- Fiber: 4.3 g
- Protein: 46 g
- Cholesterol: 188.8 mg
- Sugars: 12.6 g
- Sodium: 1254.7 mg
- Potassium: 707.9 mg

Sautéed Swiss Chard

Season your Swiss chard with butter, garlic, Parmesan cheese, and lemon juice to turn it into something that you'd look forward to having more often.

Serving Size: 4

Preparation Cooking Time: 25 minutes

Ingredients:

- 2 tablespoons olive oil
- 2 tablespoons butter
- 1 onion, chopped
- 1 tablespoon garlic, minced
- 1 cup Swiss card, chopped
- 1 tablespoon lemon juice
- ½ cup dry white wine
- Salt to taste
- 2 tablespoons Parmesan cheese, grated

Instructions:

1. Pour the oil into a pan over medium heat.

2. Stir in the butter.

3. Cook the onion and garlic for 30 seconds.

4. Stir in the Swiss chard.

5. Pour in the wine.

6. Simmer for 5 minutes.

7. Add the lemon juice.

8. Sprinkle with the salt and Parmesan cheese.

Nutrients per Serving:

- Calories: 165.3
- Fat: 13.4 g
- Saturated Fat: 5 g
- Carbohydrates: 4.9 g
- Fiber: 1.1 g
- Protein: 2.3 g
- Cholesterol: 17.5 mg
- Sugars: 1.4 g
- Sodium: 202.4 mg
- Potassium: 268 mg

Italian Meatloaf

What makes this meatloaf extra special is the thick layer of mozzarella cheese on top baked until golden.

Serving Size: 6

Preparation Cooking Time: 1 hour and 15 minutes

Ingredients:

- 1 ½ lb. ground beef
- 2 eggs, beaten
- ¾ cup breadcrumbs
- ¼ cup ketchup
- 14 oz. canned diced tomatoes
- 1 teaspoon garlic salt
- 1 teaspoon dried basil
- 1 teaspoon dried oregano
- 1 teaspoon Italian seasoning
- 2 cups mozzarella cheese, shredded and divided

Instructions:

1. Preheat your oven to 350 degrees F.

2. Combine the ground beef, eggs, breadcrumbs, ketchup, tomatoes, garlic salt, dried herbs, Italian seasoning and ½ cup mozzarella cheese.

3. Mix well.

4. Press the mixture into a loaf pan.

5. Sprinkle the remaining cheese on top of the meatloaf.

6. Cover with foil.

7. Bake in the oven for 1 hour.

Nutrients per Serving:

- Calories: 538.5
- Fat: 38.9 g
- Saturated Fat: 16.6 g
- Carbohydrates: 15.6 g
- Fiber: 1.4 g
- Protein: 29.8 g
- Cholesterol: 180.6 mg
- Sugars: 5.2 g
- Sodium: 941.3 mg
- Potassium: 385 mg

Bruschetta Chicken Bake

This recipe is a wonderful combination of baked chicken and bruschetta. It's not only delectable, but it's also easy to make. It only takes less than an hour to get this dish done.

Serving Size: 6

Preparation Cooking Time: 50 minutes

Ingredients:

- Cooking spray
- 1 ½ lb. chicken breast, sliced into cubes
- Salt to taste
- ½ cup water
- 15 oz. canned diced tomatoes, undrained
- 6 oz. bread stuffing mix (chicken flavor)
- 2 cloves garlic, minced
- 2 cups mozzarella cheese, shredded
- 1 tablespoon Italian seasoning

Instructions:

1. Preheat your oven to 400 degrees.

2. Spray your baking pan with oil.

3. Season the chicken cubes with the salt.

4. Add the chicken cubes to the baking pan.

5. Combine the water, tomatoes, stuffing mix and garlic in a bowl.

6. Spread the cheese on top of the chicken.

7. Season with the Italian seasoning.

8. Sprinkle the stuffing mixture on top.

9. Bake in the oven for 30 minutes.

Nutrients per Serving:

- Calories: 349
- Fat: 8.5 g
- Saturated Fat: 4.4 g
- Carbohydrates: 25.9 g
- Fiber: 1.8 g
- Protein: 39.2 g
- Cholesterol: 90.3 mg
- Sugars: 4.6 g
- Sodium: 1257.3 mg
- Potassium: 497.3 mg

Italian Fish Fillet

Light, filling, and full of flavor—this Italian fish fillet is sure to satisfy your taste buds. Simmer fish fillets in tomato sauce with crushed tomatoes and olives and season with garlic and herbs.

Serving Size: 6

Preparation Cooking Time: 40 minutes

Ingredients:

- 2 tablespoons olive oil
- 1 onion, sliced thinly
- 2 cloves garlic, crushed and minced
- 15 oz. canned diced tomatoes
- 1/2 cup black olives, pitted and sliced
- 1 tablespoon fresh parsley, chopped
- 1/2 cup dry white wine
- 1 lb. cod fillets

Instructions:

1. Pour the oil into a pan over medium heat.

2. Cook the onion and garlic for 2 minutes.

3. Pour in the wine.

4. Stir in the olives, tomatoes, and parsley.

5. Simmer for 5 to 7 minutes.

6. Add the fish fillets to the tomato sauce.

7. Simmer for another 5 minutes.

Nutrients per Serving:

- Calories: 230
- Fat: 9.4 g
- Saturated Fat: 1.0 g
- Carbohydrates: 8.2 g
- Fiber: 1.8 g
- Protein: 21.2 g
- Cholesterol: 41 mg
- Sugars: 4 g
- Sodium: 459 mg
- Potassium: 455 mg

Garlic Mashed Potato

Turn regular mashed potato into something more flavorful by mixing it with roasted garlic paste, herbs, salt and pepper.

Serving Size: 4

Preparation Cooking Time: 1 hour and 15 minutes

Ingredients:

- 6 cloves garlic, peeled
- ¼ cup olive oil
- 7 potatoes, sliced into cubes
- ½ cup milk
- ¼ cup Parmesan cheese, grated
- 2 tablespoons butter
- Salt and pepper to taste

Instructions:

1. Preheat your oven to 350 degrees F.

2. Add the garlic to a baking pan.

3. Drizzle with the oil.

4. Cover the pan with foil.

5. Bake in the oven for 45 minutes.

6. Boil the potatoes in a pot of water until tender.

7. Drain the potatoes and transfer to a bowl.

8. Mash the potatoes using a fork or potato masher.

9. Add the garlic to the food processor.

10. Pulse until it turns into a paste.

11. Stir the garlic into the mashed potatoes along with the rest of the ingredients.

Nutrients per Serving:

- Calories: 250.6
- Fat: 10.8 g
- Saturated Fat: 3.4 g
- Carbohydrates: 34.2 g
- Fiber: 4.2 g
- Protein: 5.4 g
- Cholesterol: 11.1 mg
- Sugars: 2.2 g
- Sodium: 222 mg
- Potassium: 821.4 mg

Turkey Meatballs with Blue Cheese

Add blue cheese to turkey meatballs to give it incredible flavors you can't find in other meatball recipes.

Serving Size: 6

Preparation Cooking Time: 1 hour

Ingredients:

- 4 cloves garlic, minced
- 1 onion, minced
- 2 jalapeno peppers, chopped
- 1 lb. ground turkey
- ½ cup breadcrumbs
- 3 tablespoons blue cheese
- 1 ½ tablespoons soy sauce
- 3 egg whites, beaten
- 3 tablespoons olive oil
- 1 tablespoon dried parsley
- 1 teaspoon chili powder
- 1 tablespoon Italian seasoning
- Pepper to taste

Instructions:

1. Preheat your oven to 400 degrees F.

2. Cover your baking pan with foil.

3. Add the garlic cloves to the food processor until minced.

4. Add the jalapeno and onion to the food processor.

5. Process for a few more seconds.

6. Add these to a bowl.

7. Stir in the rest of the ingredients.

8. Mix well.

9. Form meatballs from the mixture.

10. Add these to a baking pan.

11. Bake in the oven for 25 minutes.

Nutrients per Serving:

- Calories: 246.6
- Fat: 14.4 g
- Saturated Fat: 3.3 g
- Carbohydrates: 10.3 g
- Fiber: 1.6 g
- Protein: 19.8 g
- Cholesterol: 59.1 mg
- Sugars: 1.4 g
- Sodium: 427.6 mg
- Potassium: 287 mg

Balsamic Chicken

The sweet and savory glaze covering chicken breast fillet certainly contributes something special to the family dinner.

Serving Size: 4

Preparation Cooking Time: 45 minutes

Ingredients:

- 1 clove garlic, crushed and minced
- ½ cup chicken broth
- 1 teaspoon dried Italian herb seasoning
- ¼ cup balsamic vinegar
- 2 tablespoons sugar
- 4 chicken breast fillets
- 1 tablespoon olive oil

Instructions:

1. In a bowl, mix the garlic, chicken broth, vinegar, Italian herb seasoning and sugar.

2. Soak the chicken in this mixture and marinate for 10 minutes.

3. Flip and marinate for another 10 minutes.

4. Pour the olive oil into a pan over medium high heat.

5. Add the chicken to the pan.

6. Cook for 6 to 7 minutes per side.

7. Add the marinade into the pan.

8. Cook until the sauce has thickened.

Nutrients per Serving:

- Calories: 194.1
- Fat: 4.9 g
- Saturated Fat: 0.9 g
- Carbohydrates: 9.8 g
- Fiber: 0.2 g
- Protein: 26.4 g
- Cholesterol: 65.8 mg
- Sugars: 9.2 g
- Sodium: 79.1 mg
- Potassium: 314.8 mg

Zucchini Parmesan

Zucchini slices with tomato sauce and Parmesan cheese—this is an incredible side dish that pairs well with most main courses.

Serving Size: 4

Preparation Cooking Time: 45 minutes

Ingredients:

- Water
- 2 zucchinis, sliced thinly
- 2 tablespoons olive oil
- 2 tablespoons olive oil
- 1 onion, diced
- 2 cloves garlic, crushed and minced
- 16 oz. tomato sauce
- 4 tablespoons Parmesan cheese, grated
- 1 cup mozzarella cheese, shredded

Instructions:

1. Preheat your oven to 325 degrees F.

2. Fill a pot with water.

3. Boil the zucchini until tender.

4. Add the oil to a pan over medium heat.

5. Cook the onion and garlic for 2 minutes, stirring frequently.

6. Mix the onion, garlic, and zucchini in a baking pan.

7. Pour the tomato sauce on top of the zucchini mixture.

8. Sprinkle the Parmesan and mozzarella cheese on top.

9. Bake in the oven for 20 minutes.

Nutrients per Serving:

- Calories: 217
- Fat: 11.5 g
- Saturated Fat: 3.7 g
- Carbohydrates: 21 g
- Fiber: 4.7 g
- Protein: 8.3 g
- Cholesterol: 16.3 mg
- Sugars: 12.2 g
- Sodium: 512.3 mg
- Potassium: 681 mg

Chicken Scarpariello

Chicken thighs cooked in sweet sour sauce—this is a recipe that your family will surely ask you to make more often.

Serving Size: 2

Preparation Cooking Time: 35 minutes

Ingredients:

- 2 teaspoons butter
- 2 tablespoons olive oil
- 1 ¼ lb. chicken breast fillet
- Salt and pepper to taste
- 3 tablespoons all-purpose flour
- 2 cloves garlic, minced
- 2 tablespoons shallots, chopped
- ½ cup white wine
- 1 cup water
- ½ teaspoon dried rosemary
- 1 cube chicken bouillon

Instructions:

1. Add the butter and oil to a pan over medium heat.

2. Season the chicken with the salt and pepper.

3. Coat with flour.

4. Cook in the pan for 3 minutes per side.

5. Add the garlic and shallots to the pan.

6. Cook for 1 minute, stirring often.

7. Add the rest of the ingredients.

8. Cook for 2 to 3 minutes or until the sauce has thickened.

Nutrients per Serving:

- Calories: 580.1
- Fat: 21.4 g
- Saturated Fat: 5.4 g
- Carbohydrates: 14.3 g
- Fiber: 0.7 g
- Protein: 67.7 g
- Cholesterol: 175.8 mg
- Sugars: 1 g
- Sodium: 1085.8 mg
- Potassium: 845.8 mg

Italian Garlic Bread

Garlic bread is a classic snack that's not only easy to make, but it's also flavorful and satisfying.

Serving Size: 8

Preparation Cooking Time: 25 minutes

Ingredients:

- ½ cup butter
- 1 tablespoon dried parsley
- 1 ½ tablespoons garlic powder
- 8 oz. mozzarella cheese, shredded
- 1 loaf Italian bread, sliced

Instructions:

1. First, preheat your oven to 350 degrees F.

2. In a pan over medium heat, add the butter.

3. Stir in the parsley and garlic powder.

4. Add the bread to a baking pan.

5. Brush with the garlic butter mixture.

6. Bake in the oven for 10 minutes.

7. Sprinkle with the mozzarella cheese on top.

8. Bake for another 5 minutes.

Nutrients per Serving:

- Calories: 332.3
- Fat: 18 g
- Saturated Fat: 10.6 g
- Carbohydrates: 30.4 g
- Fiber: 1.7 g
- Protein: 12.2 g
- Cholesterol: 48.4 mg
- Sugars: 1.2 g
- Sodium: 587.6 mg
- Potassium: 113.1 mg

Baked Halibut

This is not like your regular baked fish. This one is topped with Italian veggies and feta cheese.

Serving Size: 4

Preparation Cooking Time: 30 minutes

Ingredients:

- 1 teaspoon olive oil
- 1 cup zucchini, chopped
- 1 cup onion, minced
- 2 cloves garlic, crushed and minced
- 2 cups tomatoes, diced
- 2 tablespoons fresh basil leaves, chopped
- Salt and pepper to taste
- ¼ teaspoon salt
- 4 halibut steaks
- ¼ cup feta cheese, crumbled

Instructions:

1. Preheat your oven to 450 degrees F.

2. Pour the oil into a pan over medium heat.

3. Cook the onion, garlic, and zucchini for 5 minutes.

4. Stir in the salt, pepper, basil, and tomatoes.

5. Place the fish steaks in a baking pan.

6. Top the fish with the zucchini mixture.

7. Sprinkle the feta cheese on top.

8. Bake in the oven for 15 minutes.

Nutrients per Serving:

- Calories: 258.7
- Fat: 8 g
- Saturated Fat: 2.6 g
- Protein: 38.5 g
- Carbohydrates: 6.7 g
- Fiber: 1.7 g
- Sugars: 4 g
- Cholesterol: 65.5 mg
- Sodium: 384.8 mg
- Potassium: 1089.7 mg

Salmon Pesto

Spread a layer of pesto sauce on top of salmon fillet and bake it until it's flaky and full of flavor.

Serving Size: 4

Preparation Cooking Time: 40 minutes

Ingredients:

- 2 lb. salmon fillets
- 1 tablespoon lemon juice
- 1 lemon, sliced
- 1 ½ cups pesto
- ½ cup white wine

Instructions:

1. Grease your baking pan with oil.

2. Add the salmon to the baking pan.

3. Pour the wine over the fish and drizzle with the lemon juice.

4. Marinate for 15 minutes.

5. Preheat your broiler.

6. Spread the pesto on top of the fish.

7. Broil the fish for 10 minutes.

8. Add the lemon slices on top of the fish.

9. Broil for another 5 minutes.

Nutrients per Serving:

- Calories: 241.6
- Fat: 14.4 g
- Saturated Fat: 8.4 g
- Carbohydrates: 5.4 g
- Fiber: 0.3 g
- Protein: 21.9 g
- Cholesterol: 104.7 mg
- Sugars: 0.4 g
- Sodium: 645 mg
- Potassium: 206.4 mg

Pesto Pizza

Craving for pizza? Here's a recipe you can prepare, so you can enjoy healthy and homemade pizza.

Serving Size: 6

Preparation Cooking Time: 20 minutes

Ingredients:

- 1 pizza crust
- ½ cup pesto
- 1 onion, chopped
- 2 green bell peppers, chopped
- 2 oz. black olives, drained
- 1 tomato, sliced
- 4 oz. artichoke hearts, sliced
- 1 cup feta cheese, crumbled

Instructions:

1. Preheat your oven to 450 degrees F.

2. Spread the pesto sauce on top of the pizza crust.

3. Sprinkle the veggies and cheese on top.

4. Bake in the oven for 10 minutes.

Nutrients per Serving:

- Calories: 76.9
- Fat: 1 g
- Saturated Fat: 0.2 g
- Carbohydrates: 11.8 g
- Fiber: 2.1 g
- Protein: 1.9 g
- Sugars: 7.5 g
- Cholesterol: 0 mg
- Sodium: 258.2 mg
- Potassium: 312.8 mg

Stuffed Bell Peppers

This is definitely a great idea if you're looking for an appetizer that's not only tasty and filling, but it's also easy to make.

Serving Size: 4

Preparation Cooking Time: 1 hour and 50 minutes

Ingredients:

- 2 tablespoons olive oil, divided
- 1/8 cup celery, minced
- 1/8 cup carrots, minced
- 6 bell peppers, tops sliced off
- ¼ lb. bacon, diced
- ½ lb. ground beef
- 1 cup marinara sauce
- ¼ cup red wine
- Red pepper flakes
- ¼ cup heavy cream
- ½ cup Parmesan cheese, grated and divided
- ½ cup cooked rice

Instructions:

1. Preheat your oven to 375 degrees F.

2. Pour half of the olive oil to a pan over medium heat.

3. Cook the celery and carrots for 5 minutes.

4. Add the bacon and beef.

5. Cook until brown.

6. Pour in the wine and marinara sauce.

7. Season with the red pepper flakes.

8. Stir in the Parmesan cheese, rice, and cream.

9. Simmer for 5 minutes or until liquid has been absorbed.

10. Add the peppers to a baking pan.

11. Stuff with the beef and rice mixture.

12. Drizzle with the remaining oil.

13. Bake for 30 minutes.

Nutrients per Serving:

- Calories: 310
- Fat: 20.4 g
- Saturated Fat: 8.0 g
- Cholesterol: 54 mg
- Sugars: 6 g
- Carbohydrates: 17.2 g
- Fiber: 3.1 g
- Protein: 13.7 g
- Sodium: 511 mg
- Potassium: 506 mg

Margherita Pizza

You don't have to be a vegetarian to fall in love with Margherita pizza--pizza crust topped with tomato slices, chopped basil, and melted cheese.

Serving Size: 4

Preparation Cooking Time: 45 minutes

Ingredients:

- 10 fresh basil leaves, washed, dried
- 2 cloves garlic, minced
- ¼ cup olive oil
- Salt to taste
- 8 tomatoes, sliced
- 2 baked pizza crusts
- 8 oz. Mozzarella cheese, shredded
- 4 oz. Fontina cheese, shredded
- ½ cup Parmesan cheese, grated
- ½ cup crumbled feta cheese

Instructions:

1. Combine the garlic, olive oil and salt.

2. Toss the tomatoes in this mixture.

3. Marinate for 15 minutes.

4. Preheat your oven to 400 degrees F.

5. Brush the pizza crust with tomato marinade.

6. Sprinkle with the cheese.

7. Top with the tomato mixture.

8. Add the rest of the ingredients on top of the pizza.

9. Bake in the oven for 10 minutes.

Nutrients per Serving:

- Calories: 551.4
- Fat: 25.6 g
- Saturated Fat: 11 g
- Carbohydrates: 54.4 g
- Fiber: 2.8 g
- Protein: 28.9 g
- Cholesterol: 58.4 mg
- Sugars: 4.6 g
- Sodium: 1182.5 mg
- Potassium: 200.5 mg

Panna Cotta

Panna cotta is a popular Italian dessert that's enjoyed in many parts of the world. It is made with sweetened cream with gelatin and flavored with vanilla or coffee, among other choices.

Serving Size: 6

Preparation Cooking Time: 4 hours and 15 minutes

Ingredients:

- ⅓ cup skim milk
- 1 ½ teaspoons vanilla extract
- 1 packet unflavored gelatin
- ½ cup white sugar
- 2 ½ cups heavy cream

Instructions:

1. Pour the milk into a bowl.

2. Add the gelatin powder.

3. In a pan over medium heat, combine the sugar and cream.

4. Bring to a boil.

5. Pour in the milk mixture.

6. Stir until it has been completely dissolved.

7. Cook for 1 minute, stirring frequently.

8. Add the vanilla.

9. Pour the mixture into ramekins.

10. Let cool for 5 minutes.

11. Cover with foil.

12. Refrigerate for 4 hours.

Nutrients per Serving:

- Calories: 418.3
- Fat: 36.7 g
- Saturated Fat: 22.8 g
- Carbohydrates: 20.2 g
- Fiber: 0 g
- Protein: 3.5 g
- Cholesterol: 136.1 mg
- Sugars: 17.6 g
- Sodium: 45.8 mg
- Potassium: 97.7 mg

Hazelnut Cinnamon Biscotti

Also called cantucci, biscotti is an Italian biscuit that originated from Prato, Tuscany, Italy. In this recipe, we flavor it up with cinnamon and hazelnut.

Serving Size: 4

Preparation Cooking Time: 1 hour

Ingredients:

- ¾ cup butter
- 1 ½ teaspoons vanilla extract
- 1 cup white sugar
- ¾ teaspoon baking powder
- 2 eggs
- 2 ½ cups all-purpose flour
- 1 teaspoon ground cinnamon
- Pinch salt
- 1 cup hazelnuts

Instructions:

1. Preheat your oven to 350 degrees F.

2. Line your baking pan with parchment paper.

3. In a bowl, mix the sugar and butter.

4. Mix until consistency is fluffy.

5. Add the vanilla and eggs.

6. Stir in the all-purpose flour, baking powder, cinnamon, and salt.

7. Add the hazelnuts.

8. Form logs from the dough.

9. Add the logs to the baking pan.

10. Flatten each log.

11. Bake for 30 minutes.

12. Make slices on top of the biscuits.

13. Bake for another 10 minutes, flipping once.

Nutrients per Serving:

- Calories: 138.3
- Fat: 7.8 g
- Saturated Fat: 3.2 g
- Carbohydrates: 15.5 g
- Fiber: 0.8 g
- Protein: 2.2 g
- Cholesterol: 24.6 mg
- Sugars: 6.9 g
- Sodium: 88.5 mg
- Potassium: 48.4 mg

Sausage Broccoli Pasta

Another pasta dish that you're bound to fall in love with—this one is made with cavatelli pasta tossed with broccoli and sausage.

Serving Size: 8

Preparation Cooking Time: 35 minutes

Ingredients:

- 1 lb. Italian sausage, removed from casing and crumbled
- ½ cup olive oil
- 4 cloves garlic, crushed and minced
- 16 oz. broccoli, steamed
- 16 oz. cavatelli pasta, cooked according to package directions
- ½ teaspoon red pepper flakes
- ¼ cup Parmesan cheese, grated

Instructions:

1. In a pan over medium heat, cook the sausage until brown.

2. Stir in the olive oil and garlic.

3. Cook for 1 minute, stirring frequently.

4. Stir in the cooked pasta and steamed broccoli.

5. Sprinkle with the red pepper flakes and Parmesan cheese.

Nutrients per Serving:

- Calories: 547.5
- Fat: 33 g
- Saturated Fat: 9 g
- Carbohydrates: 45.5 g
- Fiber: 3.5 g
- Protein: 18.4 g
- Cholesterol: 45.3 mg
- Sugars: 3.2 g
- Sodium: 470 mg
- Potassium: 356.1 mg

Italian Pork Tenderloin

Adding sun-dried tomatoes, cream, sage, and bacon to this pork tenderloin dish certainly deepens the flavor.

Serving Size: 4

Preparation Cooking Time: 50 minutes

Ingredients:

- 2 tablespoons olive oil
- ¼ cup bacon, chopped
- 1 white onion, chopped
- 2 tablespoons sun-dried tomatoes, sliced
- 2 tablespoons fresh parsley, chopped
- 2 tablespoons fresh sage, chopped
- ½ cup heavy cream
- ½ cup low-sodium chicken broth
- Salt and pepper to taste
- 1 ½ lb. pork tenderloin, sliced into strips

Instructions:

1. Add the oil to a pan over medium heat.

2. Cook the bacon, onion, and sun-dried tomatoes for 5 minutes.

3. Season with the parsley and sage.

4. Stir in the pork tenderloin strips.

5. Cook for another 5 minutes, stirring frequently.

6. Pour in the cream and broth.

7. Season with the salt and pepper.

8. Bring to the boil.

9. Reduce heat and simmer for 20 to 30 minutes or until the sauce has thickened.

Nutrients per Serving:

- Calories: 356
- Fat: 25 g
- Saturated Fat: 10.3 g
- Carbohydrates: 3.1 g
- Fiber: 0.5 g
- Protein: 28.9 g
- Cholesterol: 121.8 mg
- Sugars: 0.5 g
- Sodium: 390.3 mg
- Potassium: 531.2 mg

Mozzarella Tomato Bites

This is one of the easiest and simplest Italian appetizers that you can serve at home or during gatherings. But for sure, everyone will love these tasty mozzarella and tomato bites.

Serving Size: 8

Preparation Cooking Time: 20 minutes

Ingredients:

- 20 grape tomatoes, sliced in half
- 20 basil leaves
- 20 mozzarella balls
- ¼ cup olive oil
- ½ cup balsamic vinegar
- Salt and pepper to taste

Instructions:

1. Thread the tomatoes, basil leaves and mozzarella balls onto toothpicks.

2. Add to a serving plate.

3. Drizzle with the oil and vinegar.

4. Season with the salt and pepper.

Nutrients per Serving:

- Calories: 210.6
- Fat: 23.9 g
- Saturated Fat: 10.9 g
- Carbohydrates: 6.6 g
- Fiber: 1.5 g
- Protein: 17.9 g
- Cholesterol: 59.8 mg
- Sugars: 4 g
- Sodium: 627.3 mg
- Potassium: 355.2 mg

Conclusion

It's so easy to fall in love with Italian cuisine.

From pasta to pizza and everything in between, you'd surely find Italian dishes worth the time and effort.

Thanks to this book, you don't have to take a trip to Italy or dine in fancy Italian restaurants to get a taste of delicious and authentic Italian dishes.

Bounappetito!

About the Author

A native of Albuquerque, New Mexico, Sophia Freeman found her calling in the culinary arts when she enrolled at the Sante Fe School of Cooking. Freeman decided to take a year after graduation and travel around Europe, sampling the cuisine from small bistros and family owned restaurants from Italy to Portugal. Her bubbly personality and inquisitive nature made her popular with the locals in the villages and when she finished her trip and came home, she had made friends for life in the places she had visited. She also came home with a deeper understanding of European cuisine.

Freeman went to work at one of Albuquerque's 5-star restaurants as a sous-chef and soon worked her way up to head chef. The restaurant began to feature Freeman's original dishes as specials on the menu and soon after, she began to write e-books with her recipes. Sophia's dishes mix local flavours with European inspiration making them irresistible to the diners in her restaurant and the online community.

Freeman's experience in Europe didn't just teach her new ways of cooking, but also unique methods of presentation. Using rich sauces, crisp vegetables and meat cooked to perfection, she creates a stunning display as well as a delectable dish. She has won many local awards for her cuisine and she continues to delight her diners with her culinary masterpieces.

Author's Afterthoughts

I want to convey my big thanks to all of my readers who have taken the time to read my book. Readers like you make my work so rewarding and I cherish each and every one of you.

Grateful cannot describe how I feel when I know that someone has chosen my work over all of the choices available online. I hope you enjoyed the book as much as I enjoyed writing it.

Feedback from my readers is how I grow and learn as a chef and an author. Please take the time to let me know your thoughts by leaving a review on Amazon so I and your fellow readers can learn from your experience.

My deepest thanks,

Sophia Freeman

Subscribe to the Newsletter!

Your email address   Subscribe

https://sophia.subscribemenow.com/

★ ★ ★ ★ ★ ★ ★ ★ ★ ★ ★

Made in the USA
Las Vegas, NV
04 October 2024

96318330R00092